INTRODUCTION

Welcome to "The Little Book of Cricket Excuses"! Whether you're a seasoned Cricket pro or a newcomer to the feild, we've all experienced those matches when the ball just doesn't seem to bounce your way, and frustration sets in. But don't worry, because this little book is here to provide you with a delightful collection of inventive excuses for those moments when your Cricket adventures take an unexpected turn.

Cricket is a sport that demands precision, technique, and a keen understanding of the field's dynamics. However, even the most skilled players can find themselves mystified, wondering why their cover drives are off the mark or their full toss seems to lack accuracy. It's during these moments that the art of excuse-making becomes a valuable skill.

Within the pages of this book, you'll discover over 100 unique excuses that encompass the myriad of factors that can influence your Cricket performance. From weather-related challenges and equipment quirks to field conditions and distracting spectators, this book covers it all.

So, whether you're in search of a witty response to placate your Cricket buddies or simply looking for a bit of humor to lighten the mood after a challenging match, "The Little Book of Cricket Excuses" is your go-to source. Let this collection of excuses remind you that, even on those days when your Cricket game feels a bit off, the joy of being on the field and the anticipation of your next six are always worth it.

So sit back, take a breather, and remember that sometimes the most entertaining part of the game is crafting the perfect excuse!

Enjoy your time on the Cricket field, and may your stories of Cricket mishaps and triumphs be a source of laughter and camaraderie for years to come!

Ace O'Blame

TABLE OF
CONTENTS

CHAPTER 1: EXCUSE DELIVERY

Welcome to "The Little Book of Cricket Excuses," where we take the art of excuse-making to new heights. In this section, we'll equip you with the skills needed to deliver Cricket excuses with a straight face and a twinkle in the eye.

Let's dive into some invaluable tips for delivering Cricket excuses with just the right touch of humor:

Maintain a Deadpan Expression: Picture this: you're delivering your excuse with a completely serious face, as if your explanation is the most rational thing in the world. By maintaining a deadpan expression, you'll create a delightful contrast between the seriousness of your delivery and the absurdity of the excuse itself.

Use Dramatic Pause: Before you unveil your excuse, pause for a brief moment. Let the anticipation build, and create an aura of intrigue around your explanation. This dramatic pause will heighten the comedic effect, leaving your fellow players eagerly awaiting your excuse.

Example: "You won't believe it, but just as I was about to hit a six, a mischievous butterfly landed on my bat and whispered, 'Try a leg pull, my friend!' How could I ignore such wise counsel?"

Emphasize with Hand Gestures: Adding animated hand gestures to your storytelling can make your excuse come to life. Mimic the motions of your Cricket shots, or even imaginary Cricket ball trajectories to inject a playful element into your excuse.

These tips will help you deliver Cricket excuses with impeccable timing and style. Get ready to turn those challenging moments on the field into opportunities for laughter and camaraderie!

Maintain a Twinkle in the Eye: While explaining your excuse with a serious demeanor, let your eyes twinkle with mischief and shared amusement. This subtle sparkle signals to your Cricket companions that you're all in on the playful moment.

Example: "Ah, that missed shot? Well, you see, the Cricket balls in these parts have developed a mischievous streak. They enjoy taking unexpected detours, much to the surprise of players like me!"

Play with Sarcasm: Infuse your excuse with a touch of sarcasm to deliver it in a tongue-in-cheek manner. Use irony to signal to your fellow Cricket players that you're fully aware of the humorous nature of your explanation.

Example: "Of course, I intentionally hit the ball into the wicket. It's part of my top-secret strategy to keep the umpire from feeling lonely. Someone's got to pay them some attention!"

Employ a Touch of Irony: As you share your excuse, add a hint of irony to your tone to underscore the delightful absurdity of the situation. This dry humor will let your Cricket buddies know that you're crafting an excuse with a playful wink.

Example: "I aimed for the boundary, but you see, the Cricket field is a stage for unpredictable dramas. The ball decided to pursue a career in acting and dramatically pulled up short."

Remember, the essence of delivering Cricket excuses with a straight face and a twinkle in the eye is to blend earnestness with a playful spirit. Practice these tips, adapt them to your personal style, and revel in the laughter and camaraderie they bring to your Cricket adventures!

Ace O'Blame

"I want my son to become
Sachin Tendulkar."

BRIAN LARA

CHAPTER 2:
THE
EXCUSES:
RELATABLE

Weather Interruptions: Unfavorable weather conditions like heavy rain, intense heat, strong winds, or extreme cold can significantly impact my performance on the cricket field. For example, rain can make the pitch slippery, while extreme heat can lead to exhaustion.

Lack of Focus: Factors such as excessive noise, ground maintenance, or distractions from fellow players can disrupt my concentration and hinder my gameplay. These distractions can make it challenging to stay focused during the match.

Poor Pitch Conditions: If the cricket pitch is wet, muddy, or in poor condition, it becomes difficult to maintain proper footing and execute shots effectively. This can result in unforced errors and frustration.

Equipment Issues: Any problems with my cricket bat, ball, or protective gear can significantly impact my ability to perform at my best. For instance, a damaged bat can result in erratic shots.

Injuries: Sudden injuries, such as the shoulder, knee, or back, can restrict my mobility and shot accuracy. Playing through pain can be challenging and affect my performance.

Lack of Practice: Not having enough practice or time on the field recently can lead to rusty skills and mistimed shots. Consistent practice is essential for maintaining cricketing proficiency.

Facing a Skilled Opponent: Sometimes, the opposing team simply plays exceptionally well, making it difficult for our team to keep up. Competing against a highly skilled opponent can be a tough challenge.

Mental Fatigue: Mental exhaustion or stress can influence my decision-making and concentration during a match. A distracted mindset can lead to errors on the field.

Inadequate Warm-up: Insufficient warm-up or preparation before the game can result in slow reactions and stiffness. A proper warm-up is crucial to perform at my best in cricket.

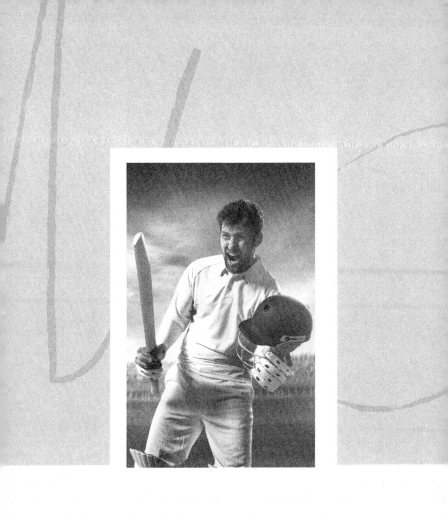

"You don't win or lose the games because of the 11 you select. You win or lose with what those 11 do on the field."

RAHUL DRAVID

Unfamiliar Pitch: Playing on an unfamiliar cricket pitch or in an unfamiliar stadium can disrupt my performance.

Umpire's Decision Dilemma: Sometimes, the decisions made by the umpire can be quite perplexing. When a questionable call doesn't go my way, it can be mentally challenging to regain composure and perform at my best. It's like trying to hit a moving target.

Unpredictable Toss Outcome: The toss is a game-changer, and losing it can set the tone for the entire match. We were at the mercy of the coin, and unfortunately, it didn't fall in our favor today.

Opponent's Mental Tactics: My opponent might use psychological tactics, such as sledging or strategic timeouts, to distract me and break my concentration during the game.

Lingering Injury Effects: Even if I've recovered from an injury, I might not be at my best due to residual physical discomfort or fear of re-injury.

Spectator Disturbances: Unexpected noises or disturbances from the crowd, like cheering, jeering, or mobile phones ringing, can disrupt my focus and affect my gameplay.

Diet or Nutrition: Poorly timed meals or unfamiliar foods can lead to discomfort or a lack of energy during a match. This can negatively impact my performance.

Travel Fatigue: Frequent travel for tournaments can result in jet lag, sleep disturbances, and general fatigue, affecting my physical and mental state on the field.

Pressure and Expectations: High-pressure situations, such as playing in front of a large audience or facing a must-win match, can lead to nervousness and uncharacteristic mistakes.

Slow Outfield: A slow and damp outfield can reduce the speed of the ball after it's hit, preventing boundaries and frustrating batters who expect a faster outfield.

Bat Condition: Changes in bat condition can impact the control and feel of my shots. If the condition isn't just right, it can lead to mishits and a loss of precision.

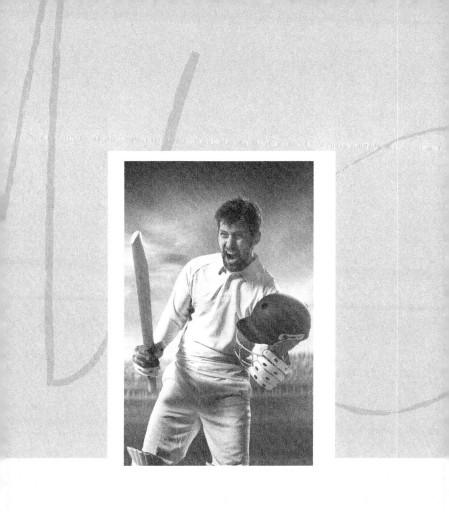

"When you play Test cricket, you don't give the Englishmen an inch. Play it tough, all the way. Grind them into the dust."

SIR DON BRADMAN

Old Cricket Balls: Some players blame the use of older cricket balls, claiming that they don't swing or grip the pitch well enough. They argue that newer balls offer better performance.

Pitch Conditions: Complaining about the pitch conditions, such as uneven bounce, cracks, or excessive turn, can be a common excuse.

Pitch Deterioration: Batting second on a pitch that deteriorates over time can make it challenging to score runs. Footmarks left by bowlers in the first innings can assist spinners and make batting a struggle.

Late Arrival: If a player arrives late due to traffic or other delays, they might use this as an excuse for not being mentally prepared or warmed up properly.

Bad Luck: At times, players attribute their performance to bad luck, like edges just missing fielders or narrowly missing the stumps.

Teammate's Performance: In cricket, players might blame their teammates for not contributing effectively or missing key plays.

Time of Day: Excuses related to the time of day are common. Some players claim they perform better during certain times of the day and blame their performance on playing during their less optimal time.

Opponent's Gamesmanship: Accusing opponents of gamesmanship, such as excessive appealing or distracting behavior, can be a way to explain poor performance.

Toss Misjudgment: Occasionally, we make the wrong call during the toss, misjudging the conditions or misreading the pitch. It's a game of chance, after all.

Unpredictable Weather: Cricket can be challenging when faced with unpredictable weather conditions, such as rain interruptions, windy conditions, or extreme heat, which can affect batting, bowling, and fielding.

Rapid Ball Movement: Swift movement of the cricket ball, such as extreme swing or seam, can make it hard to control shots or maintain line and length, reducing a player's chances of success.

"In cricket, as in life, it is often the case that the most difficult delivery to play is the one that comes very easy."

DAVID GOWER

Fatigue From Previous Match: Cricketers might attribute their performance to exhaustion from a previous match or practice session, arguing they didn't have ample time to recuperate.

Unsuitable Pitch Conditions: When playing on a pitch with different characteristics than usual (e.g., transitioning from a spin-friendly wicket to a pace-friendly one), some players might use this as an explanation for their subpar performance.

Opponent's Intimidation: Cricket is as much a psychological game, and some players might excuse their performance by citing the intimidating reputation or demeanor of their opponent.

Ball Swing and Bounce: Complaining about the movement or bounce of the cricket ball can be an excuse. Some players prefer more or less movement based on their playing style.

Dominant Opponent: If my opponent is playing exceptionally well, there's not much I can do. They're simply in superior form.

Miscommunication in Field Placement: There was a miscommunication regarding field placements and strategies within the team. This confusion led to gaps in the field and allowed the opposition to capitalize on scoring opportunities.

Inadequate Net Session: Blaming an insufficient net session for not warming up properly can be an excuse for sluggish play.

Unfavorable Crowd: Some players might lament that the crowd is too loud or distracting, affecting their concentration and performance.

Umpire's Position Predicament: The umpire's positioning can sometimes obstruct my view of the field, making it challenging to track the ball or field effectively.

Equipment Changes: Players may contend that recent alterations in their gear, such as a new bat or shoes, are negatively impacting their game.

Opponent's Defensive Tactics: Occasionally, your opponent's defensive strategies can be extremely effective. They persistently thwart your shots, making it challenging to accumulate runs.

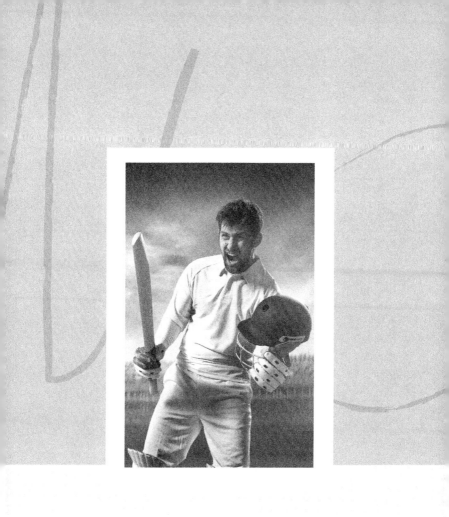

"Cricket is a pressure game, and when it comes to an India–Pakistan match, the pressure is doubled."

IMRAN KHAN

Injured Hand/Wrist: Claiming an injured hand or wrist can explain difficulties with gripping the bat, fielding, or throwing.

Glaring Sunlight: Blaming the harsh sunlight for poor play is common, especially when batting or fielding. The sun's glare can make it challenging to see the ball accurately and judge its trajectory.

Heavy Bat: Complaining about using a heavy bat suggests that your equipment hindered your performance. It's a subtle way to admit that your skills are better than your gear.

Uncomfortable Cricket Shoes: Uncomfortable or ill-fitting cricket shoes can lead to blisters or discomfort during play, impacting your performance.

Stiff Muscles: Stiff or tight muscles can limit your range of motion and affect your agility on the pitch. This excuse implies that your body wasn't in peak condition.

New Cricket Ball: Some players struggle when using a new cricket ball, as it can behave differently from older ones. This excuse points to the ball as the culprit for any erratic behavior.

Umpire's Experience Levels: Umpires with varying levels of experience may interpret situations differently. Facing an inexperienced umpire can introduce an element of unpredictability.

Incorrect Shot Selection: Selecting the wrong type of shot can lead to unsuccessful plays. Picking a shot that doesn't suit the situation or the bowler's style can result in unforced errors.

Lack of Adaptability: Our team struggled to adapt to changing conditions on the field. This lack of adaptability made it difficult to respond effectively to the opposition's tactics.

"There are two types of
batsmen in the world.
One, Sachin Tendulkar.
Two, all the others."

ANDY FLOWER

Wind Conditions: Blaming strong winds can disrupt the trajectory and speed of the cricket ball. This excuse implies that the wind was unfavorable for your performance.

Late-Night Match: Citing fatigue from a late-night cricket match shifts responsibility to external scheduling factors, suggesting that the late hour affected your game.

Rusty Skills: Acknowledging rusty skills due to a lack of practice can account for a subpar cricket performance, attributing your struggles to a lack of preparation.

Nervousness: Nerves can impact anyone's cricket game. This excuse hints that anxiety or nervousness played a significant role in your performance.

Slippery Outfield: After rain or dew settles on the outfield, it can become treacherously slippery. Fielders may struggle to maintain balance while chasing the ball, resulting in slips and fumbles.

Opponent's Bowling Style: Some cricketers make excuses about their opponent's bowling style. They might say, "I can't handle spinners," referring to opponents who specialize in spin bowling. This excuse shifts blame for a poor performance to the opponent's tactics.

Outfield Size: The size of the outfield can vary from one ground to another. Adjusting to a larger or smaller outfield can affect a fielder's positioning and lead to misjudgments when fielding.

Failure to Read Pitch Conditions: We misjudged the pitch conditions, leading to poor shot selection and ineffective bowling strategies. This lack of understanding about the pitch hindered our overall game plan.

Sledging: Mental distractions can be a convenient excuse in cricket. Players might mention that they were distracted by factors like the opponent's sledging. This type of excuse redirects attention away from their own performance.

"To me, cricket is a simple game. Keep it simple and just go out and play."

SHANE WARNE

New Technique: If you're struggling with a particular aspect of your cricket game, such as your batting technique or bowling accuracy, this excuse demonstrates your commitment to refining your skills and your willingness to experiment with new approaches.

Out of Form: This excuse is ideal when you're having difficulty focusing or simply not performing at your best. It's a candid acknowledgment that even top players occasionally face periods of inconsistency.

Bumpy Outfield: Some cricket grounds have uneven or bumpy outfields. These irregularities can cause the ball to bounce unexpectedly, making it difficult for fielders to judge its path accurately.

Challenging Opponent: Use this excuse when you're facing an opponent with a significantly different playing style than you're accustomed to. It underscores your awareness of the unique challenges posed by your adversary and your efforts to adapt to the situation.

Off Day: This straightforward excuse is effective in cricket as well. It reveals your honesty and willingness to admit when you're not performing at your peak.

Playing For Enjoyment: If you're not taking the game too seriously or are simply looking to have fun, this excuse demonstrates your positive attitude and lack of excessive pressure to win.

Struggling With Bowling: This is a classic cricket excuse suitable for players of all levels. It's forthright and acknowledges the occasional difficulties everyone encounters in delivering consistent deliveries.

Battling With Batting: Another common excuse for cricket players of all levels. It specifies the particular area of your game that requires improvement, showing your awareness of the need for better batting.

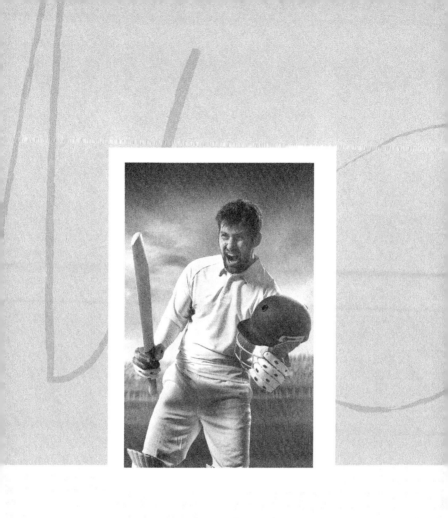

"I have witnessed Sachin (Tendulkar) playing for 24 years and have to say, that I have not seen any other cricketer play so perfectly."

SIR DON BRADMAN

Rain-Induced Duckworth-Lewis: Sudden rain interruptions invoked the Duckworth-Lewis Method, altering our required run rate dramatically. It's challenging to adapt to rapidly changing targets when the weather's unpredictability takes center stage.

Home Team's Advantage: The home team often tailors the pitch conditions to their strengths, further putting us at a disadvantage.

Unfamiliar Cricket Balls: Players might say that they struggled because the cricket balls used in the match were new and didn't suit their playing style.

Tough Opponents: In tournaments, players might argue that they had to face strong opponents early in the competition, making it difficult for them.

Pre-Match Distractions: Personal distractions or stress before a match can lead to excuses about not being mentally prepared to perform well in cricket.

Late Night: Players who had a late night or insufficient sleep may blame fatigue for their performance in cricket matches.

Bad Luck: Sometimes, players simply blame bad luck, ascribing their cricket performance to unfortunate circumstances or events during the game.

Lacking Peak Performance: This is a straightforward excuse used to explain any poor performance in cricket. It implies that the player didn't bring their best game to the field.

Heavy Meal: Eating a heavy meal before a cricket match can make a player feel sluggish and tired, affecting their agility and performance. It's best to opt for a light, energy-boosting meal.

Wicket Keeper's Call: Communication is vital in cricket, and sometimes, misunderstandings between the wicket-keeper and fielders can result in fielding errors. Confusion over who should take a catch or field the ball can lead to missed opportunities.

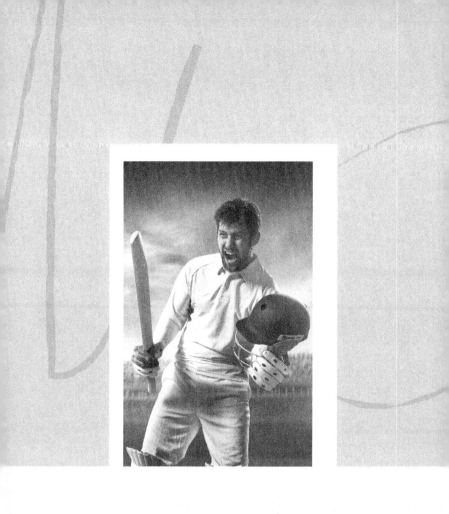

"Cricket is a most precarious profession;
it is called a team game but, in fact, no
one is so lonely as a batsman facing a
bowler supported by ten fieldsmen and
observed by two umpires to ensure that
his error does not go unpunished."

JOHN ARLOTT

Opponents Playing Too Well: Sometimes, you have to acknowledge your opponent's exceptional performance. If they're in top form, there's little you can do.

Bad Errors: Mistakes happen to everyone, but they can be particularly costly in cricket. A few errors can change the course of a game.

Ball Tampering Scandals: Sometimes, bowlers find themselves in the middle of ball tampering controversies, which can distract them from their game. The pressure and scrutiny that come with such allegations can be mentally draining and negatively impact their bowling accuracy.

Preoccupied With Upcoming Match: Staying focused on the current game is crucial, but sometimes it's challenging to avoid thinking about the next one. Being distracted by future matches can lead to errors in the present game.

Team Chemistry Issues: Bowlers require a collaborative effort from their fielding team to execute successful strategies. If there's a lack of communication or understanding among teammates, it can disrupt planned tactics and lead to poor performance on the field.

Pitch Too Slow Or Fast: Adjusting to the pitch's speed can be tricky. If you're used to fast pitches, adapting to a slow one, or vice versa, can result in unforced errors and frustration.

Ball Quality Inconsistent: The quality of cricket balls can significantly impact the game. Overly bouncy balls can be challenging to handle, while flat ones may behave unpredictably.

Battling Nerves: Even the best cricketers experience nervousness occasionally. It's natural to feel anxious before a significant match. Nervousness can hinder concentration and performance.

Feeling Unwell: If you're unwell or fatigued, playing at your best can be challenging. This is a legitimate excuse, but it's best to use it sparingly.

"Cricket is in the blood of Pakistanis, and I made sure to contribute to my country through cricket."

WASIM AKRAM

Footwork Needs Improvement: This excuse is ideal when you're struggling with your footwork, whether it's not moving into position quickly or failing to get your feet correctly aligned for shots. It reflects your awareness of the issue and your commitment to rectifying it.

Lacking Depth in Shot Placement: This excuse is suitable if you're consistently hitting the ball too short or without enough power. It demonstrates your recognition of the problem and your efforts to adjust your shot placement.

Difficulty Reading the Bowler's Deliveries: This excuse works well when you're having trouble reading the bowler's deliveries and reacting effectively. It shows that you acknowledge the challenge and are working on improving your focus.

Struggling with Yorkers: This excuse is applicable when you find it challenging to execute clean and consistent hits on Yorkers. It indicates your awareness of the issue and your commitment to enhancing your batting skills.

Not Seizing Opportunities: This excuse is fitting if you're being too passive, defensive, or missing chances to play aggressive shots. It demonstrates your awareness of missed opportunities and your intention to be more proactive.

Making Tactical Errors: This excuse is suitable when you're making tactical mistakes or not placing your shots effectively. It shows your awareness of the problem and your determination to make better decisions on the field.

Struggling with Timing: This excuse covers a range of timing-related issues, from not making clean contact with the ball to bowling run up issues.

Lacking Patience in Play: This excuse is ideal for moments when you're rushing your shots or not waiting for the right opportunities to execute them.

Insufficient power on Shots: This excuse can be used when your shots lack the required power, causing them to go short of the intended area.

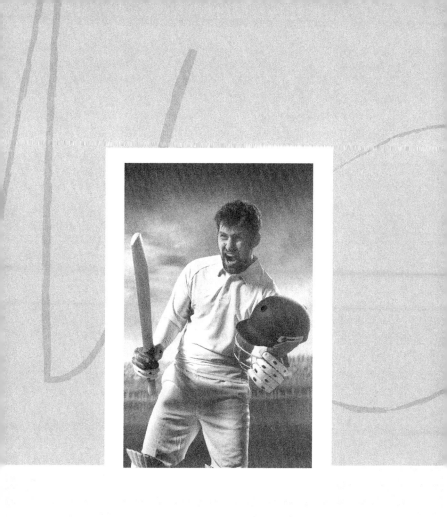

"Cricket is a game that demands respect. If you don't respect the game, it won't respect you."

SACHIN TENDULKAR

Crowded Playing Conditions: Playing cricket when the pitch or field is crowded with spectators or other matches can be distracting and challenging to concentrate.

Not Playing Aggressively Enough: This excuse is perfect to use if you're playing too passively or defensively. It shows that you're aware of your playing style and trying to make an adjustment.

Time Constraints: Some cricketers claim they didn't have enough time to prepare or warm up properly. This excuse suggests that with more time, they would have performed better.

Too Many Mistakes: This general excuse can be used to account for a subpar performance. It reflects your honesty and recognition of the errors made during the match.

Over-Focused on Opponent: Focusing too much on the weaknesses of the opponent in cricket can distract a player from their own game plan, leading to mistakes and poor performance

Heavy Kit: My kit felt like it weighed a ton today, every movement was sluggish.

Lack Of Footing Grip: My spikes lost their grip halfway through the match, kept slipping everywhere.

Poor Footwork: My footwork today resembled a drunken octopus on roller skates

Poor Bowling Grip: The ball kept slipping out of my hand, felt like I was bowling with buttered fingers.

Captain's Conundrums: Fielding placements? More like a game of pin the tail on the donkey today.

Captain's Conundrums: The pre-match team talk must have backfired, everyone seems confused

Captain's Conundrums: Bowling changes? Tried everything in the bag, but nothing seemed to work.

"The cricket field is my canvas, and the bat is my brush."

BRIAN LARA

CHAPTER 3: THE EXCUSES: A LITTLE MORE FAR FETCHED!

Dazzling Sunlight: "I couldn't focus on the ball due to the blinding sunlight. It felt like trying to play cricket on the surface of the sun!"

Bouncy Pitch: "The pitch had too much bounce. It felt like I was batting on a trampoline out there."

Erratic Wind: "The wind was incredibly tricky today, constantly changing directions at the worst moments, making it impossible to judge the ball's path."

Lifeless Cricket Ball: "Those cricket balls must have been lifeless. It was like trying to hit a brick wall with my bat."

Avian Distraction: "I got distracted by a noisy bird in the field. It was like a feathered cheerleader with perfect timing for its squawks."

Hay Fever Attack: "My allergies suddenly flared up during the match. Sneezing and batting don't mix well."

Slippery Bat Grip: "My bat grip started slipping mid-stroke. I had to play the last few overs with a bat that had suddenly turned into a bar of soap."

Mysterious Pitch Imperfection: "There was an unexplainable bump on the pitch that made me lose my balance at the worst moment. I think it's the cricket pitch fairies at work again."

Butterfly Encounter: "A butterfly fluttered in front of me just as I was about to hit a boundary. I couldn't decide whether to swat it away or go for the shot."

Rebellious Cricket Ball: "The cricket balls seemed to have a mind of their own, defying physics with unexpected bounces, as if they were plotting a revolution."

Telepathic Opponent: "My opponent must be telepathic. They always seemed to anticipate my shots before I played them."

Mysterious Mist: "A sudden and unexplained mist rolled in, turning the cricket field into a scene from a spooky cricket thriller. I couldn't see a thing."

"Cricket is a sport of the mind. You've got to be in the right frame of mind to play it."

MAHELA JAYAWARDENE

Pitch Invaders: "Suddenly, a group of rogue crickets invaded the pitch. It was like they had their own cricket match going on right in the middle of mine!"

Helmet Hijinks: "My helmet decided it needed a break. It slipped down over my eyes just as the bowler was about to release the ball. I was basically playing blindfolded."

Butterfingers Syndrome: "I suffered from a severe case of 'butterfingers syndrome.' It was as if my hands were coated in butter, and I couldn't hold onto the ball to save my life."

Umpire's Miscalculation: "The umpire seemed to have some kind of miscalculation disorder. Wide balls were called 'ins' and 'outs,' and I didn't know whether I was coming or going."

Sudden Duck Invasion:
"Out of nowhere, a group of ducks decided to waddle onto the field. I had to dodge them while trying to focus on the bowler. Quack-tastrophe!"

Boundary Line Mirage:
"The boundary line appeared to be a mirage. I kept thinking I hit a six, only to find the ball safely in the fielder's hands. It was a boundary illusion."

Inexplicable Stump Shyness: "The stumps suddenly became shy and elusive. No matter how hard I tried, I couldn't get the ball to dislodge those bashful bails."

Mischievous Squirrel Fielding: "A playful squirrel decided to join the fielding team. It darted around, distracting everyone, and even made off with the ball a few times."

Phantom Spin Wizardry:
"The ball seemed to have a mind of its own, performing acrobatics in mid-air. It spun and swerved like it was auditioning for a magic show."

Tea Break Urgency: "Just as I was about to take a crucial catch, the tea break siren went off. I had to abandon the catch to make a dash for the tea stand. Priorities!"

Ball Tampering by Birds: "A flock of cheeky crows swooped down and tampered with the ball. It swung like a boomerang, and I couldn't control it."

Gravitational Wobble: "I swear, there was a gravitational wobble on the pitch today. My yorkers became moonshots, and my spin deliveries barely hugged the ground."

"Cricket is more than just a game; it is a way of life."

RAHUL DRAVID

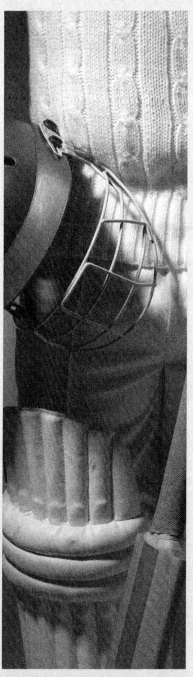

Mind-Reading Umpire: "It felt like the umpire had access to my thoughts. Every time I contemplated an LBW appeal, they signaled it without me uttering a word."

Mysterious Boundary Disappearance: "One of my well-timed shots mysteriously vanished into a Bermuda Triangle-like void in the outfield. I hope it's enjoying a tropical holiday somewhere."

Pigeon Invasion: "A squadron of pigeons decided to stage an invasion of the field during our match. They were like fielding generals, fiercely guarding their territory."

Cricket Ball Whisperer: "My opponent seemed to have a cricket ball whisperer in the stands, telepathically guiding each delivery. No wonder they always hit the target!"

Balletic Ball Bounces:
"The cricket balls seemed to have taken ballet lessons. They were gracefully pirouetting and leaping like ballerinas before reaching the batsman."

Time-Traveling Opponent: "I'm convinced my opponent had a time machine. They were both at the crease and the boundary simultaneously, hitting every ball effortlessly."

Sudden Ball Expansion: "During the game, the cricket balls appeared to inflate spontaneously. It was like trying to hit shots with beach balls!"

Cricket Ball Revolt: "The cricket balls united and demanded to be bowled gently this time. It was a peaceful protest against fast deliveries."

Overenthusiastic Fan Cheers: "There was this one fan in the stands who couldn't contain their excitement. They kept yelling 'Bravo!' every time I bowled. It was like having my personal cheer squad."

Pitchside Construction: "There was construction work going on near the pitch, and I believe the vibrations from those bulldozers affected my batting stance."

Sudden Rain of Cricket Balls: "Out of the blue, it started raining cricket balls on the field. It felt like a cricket ball meteor shower, and I couldn't find a safe spot to field."

Specter Umpires: "The umpires mysteriously vanished, and the field was haunted by mischievous spirits who kept changing the rules. It was like playing cricket in the twilight zone."

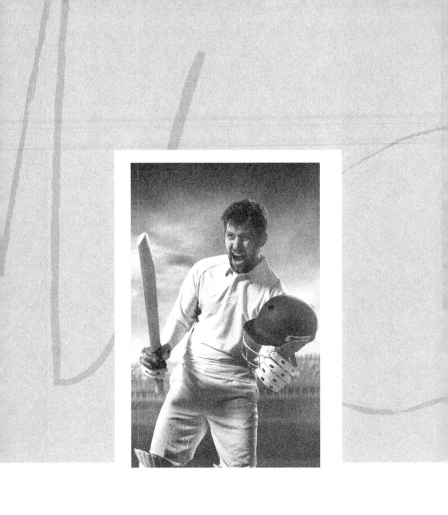

"Cricket is a team sport, but it's also about individual performances. It's a beautiful blend of both."

SUNIL GAVASKAR

Sudden Bat Swap: "My bat mysteriously switched with my teammate's mid-game. I didn't realize until I played a cover drive with a completely different bat!"

Cricket Ball Hypnosis: "The cricket balls seemed to have hypnotic powers. I couldn't take my eyes off them, and my bowling turned into a mesmerizing dance routine."

Instant Pitch Relocation: "I swear the pitch moved during the match. It was in one place for my deliveries and another for my yorkers. I need a GPS for cricket pitches!"

Time-Traveling Cricket Ball: "One of the cricket balls appeared to have its own time machine. It would teleport into the future, causing me to bowl where the ball used to be."

Umpire's Cricket Fever:
"The umpire seemed to be indulging in snacks during the match. Every time I bowled, they'd declare, 'That's a tasty delivery!'"

Holographic Cricket Ball Mirage: "A holographic illusion of cricket balls appeared on the pitch, making it impossible to pick the real deliveries from the illusions."

Cricket Ball Eclipse: "A rare cricket ball eclipse occurred just as I was delivering a googly. It was like trying to bowl to a moving shadow."

Time-Traveling Cricket Shoes: "My cricket shoes experienced a temporal glitch. One shoe was stuck in the past while the other was in the future, making it a balancing act while fielding."

Umpire's Lucky Coin:
"The umpire had a lucky coin that they kept flipping before every decision. It always seemed to land in favor of the other team. I suspect some coin-toss trickery!"

Pitch-Adjacent Cyclone:
"I'm convinced there was a miniature cyclone swirling just beside the pitch. It whisked away all our well-placed shots and carried them to fielders."

Cricket Ball Mirage: "A mirage of cricket balls appeared on the pitch, confusing our batsmen. It was like playing cricket in a desert of illusions."

Umpire's Lucky Charm: "The umpire had a lucky charm bracelet, and they'd twirl it whenever a close call came up. It mysteriously brought good fortune to our opponents."

"The real cricket is in the test of character, not just the test matches."

VIRENDER SEHWAG

Cricket Ball Conspiracy:
"The cricket balls
conspired against us,
executing mysterious
swings and spins that
defied the laws of physics.
It was a cricket ball
rebellion!"

Synchronized Cricket
Shoes: "Our cricket shoes
seemed to synchronize
their squeaking with the
bowler's run-up. We
unintentionally composed a
symphony of squeaks that
echoed through the
stadium."

Invisible Boundary Barrier:
"An invisible boundary
barrier surrounded the
field, causing our powerful
shots to bounce back into
the field of play. It was like
cricket against an unseen
force."

Cricket Ball Mind Control:
"I'm convinced the cricket
balls had telepathic
powers. They influenced
our batsmen to make
questionable shot
selections, leading to easy
catches."

Cricket Ball Tornado: "A cricket ball tornado swept across the field, sending deliveries spinning out of control. It was like trying to bat in the midst of a whirlwind."

Cricket Ball Rebellion: "The cricket balls protested for shorter matches, demanding more rest time between deliveries. They even rolled away if bowled too frequently, insisting on better work-life balance!"

Cricket Ball Euphoria: "The cricket balls entered a state of euphoria, swinging wildly with each delivery. It was as if they were dancing to their own rhythm."

Cricket Ball Acrobat: "The cricket balls transformed into acrobats, spinning and somersaulting through the air. It felt like I was playing cricket in a circus."

CHAPTER 4: A FEW CRICKET JOKES

As I stared at the Cricket Ball I kept wondering why it was getting larger and larger. And then it hit me!

Why are all the major cricket grounds around the world so cool? Because they are packed full of fans!

Why are cricketers so good at ironing? Because they all know how to spot a crease!

Why was the cricketer called a superhero? Because he is Bat-man!

Why was the cricket player wearing armor? Because he was going out to play a Knight games!

I know a retired cricket umpire. And he doesn't lift a finger now.

Why did the cricket team carry a lighter?
Because they lost all the matches!

Never drive a car like cricket is played.
Otherwise it will be a case of hit and run!

Why don't grasshoppers like football?
Because they prefer cricket!

Why did the cricketer bring a ball of string to the game?
In case he needed to 'tie' the score!

What do cricket players and car salesmen have n common?
They're both good with the pitch.

Why does a bad fielder never get ill?
Because he can't catch anything.

Wife: Have you seen the dog bowl?
Husband: No, didn't realise he played cricket!

I knew cricketer that took an IQ test.
Trouble was he got stumped straight away!

Which animal is always present in a game of cricket? A bat!

I once went out to a nightclub with a batsman who struggles with short-pitched deliveries?
Wasn't long before they got in a tangle with the bouncer.

Why are deep fielders always well-behaved? Because they know where their boundaries are.

Did you hear about the Cricket that fell in love?.
They got bowled over.

Why didn't the cricket team believe what their Captain said? Because he always had a silly point.

Why did the Cricket Captain take his team fishing?
To ensure they caught something!

'Why do you look so upset?'
'The doctor said that I can't play cricket.'
'I didn't know he had seen you play.'

A batsman scored two runs in an inning. That's when his Captain said 'Wonderful shot!'. Batsman: Which one? Captain: The one where you hit the ball!

My partner said she will leave me due to my obsession with cricket. It really knocked me for six!

Why was the batsman's delivery left on his doorstep?
Because he was out!

Why did the midwife always get to open the batting?
Because she was the best at fast deliveries.

A class were asked to write an essay on a cricket match. All the students were busy writing except one. when asked why they said 'no match due to heavy rain'.

Cricketer: "Please help me, I think I am a cricket ball".
Doctor: "How's that"
Cricketer: "Please don't you start"

Cricketer 1: The local team wants me to play for them really bad.
Cricketer 2: In which case there's no one better than you for the job!

The meaning of the word optimism?
A poor batsman applying sunscreen before coming out to bat.

"In cricket, there's always
another game, another chance.
That's what makes it so special."

RICKY PONTING

CHAPTER 5:
CRICKET
FACTS &
STATS

Sir Garfield Sobers: Was the first top-flight Cricketer to hit six consecutive sixes in one over on 31st August 1968.

Fastest Century: AB de Villiers holds the record for the fastest century in One Day Internationals (ODIs), reaching his century in just 31 balls against the West Indies in 2015.

Sachin Tendulkar's Records: Sachin Tendulkar, often called the "God of Cricket," has scored 100 international centuries and is the highest run-scorer in both Tests and ODIs.

Jim Laker's 19 Wickets: In 1956, English cricketer Jim Laker took 19 wickets in a single test match against Australia.

Brian Lara's 400 Not Out: Brian Lara from the West Indies scored 400 not out in a test match against England in 2004, setting the record for the highest individual score in Test cricket.

Muttiah Muralitharan's 1,347 Wickets: Sri Lankan bowler Muttiah Muralitharan holds the record for the most international wickets across all formats.

Sir Don Bradman's 99.94 Average: Australian cricketer Sir Don Bradman's test batting average of 99.94 is considered one of the greatest records in sports history.

First World Cup Winners: The West Indies won the first two ICC Cricket World Cups in 1975 and 1979.

Highest Total in a Test Innings: Sri Lanka holds the record for the highest team total in a Test innings, scoring 952/6 against India in 1997.

Youngest Test Debutant: Hasan Raza from Pakistan is the youngest player to debut in Test cricket, making his debut at the age of 14 years and 227 days in 1996.

Longest Test Match: The longest Test cricket match in history was from 3-14 March 1939. It was played between South Africa and England in 1939 and had to be abandoned to allow the England team to catch their boat home.

The highest individual international score in T20 cricket: 172 runs, achieved by Aaron Finch of Australia. He achieved this remarkable feat during a match against Zimbabwe in a tri-series, scoring 172 runs off just 76 deliveries

First Official International Cricket Match: The first officially recognized international cricket match was played between the United States and Canada in 1844.

Garry Sobers' All-Round Feat: West Indies cricketer Sir Garry Sobers is the only player to score six sixes in a single over in first-class cricket. He also scored 365 not out in a Test match against Pakistan in 1958, a record that stood for 36 years.

Cricket's Inception: Cricket is believed to have originated in the 16th century in England, and the first recorded cricket match took place in 1646.

Highest Team Score in an ODI: England scored 498/4 in 50 overs against Netherlands on 17 June 2022

Women's Cricket: Women's cricket has been played since the late 18th century. The first Women's World Cup was held in 1973, two years before the first Men's World Cup.

Most Ducks in Test Cricket: Courtney Walsh, the West Indian fast bowler, holds the record for the most ducks in Test cricket, with 43.

Most Sixes in T20 Internationals: Rohit Sharma of India holds the record for the most sixes in T20 Internationals, with 182 sixes to his name.

Most Sixes in a Single ODI Match: Eoin Morgan, the captain of the England cricket team, smashed 17 sixes in a single ODI match against Afghanistan in the 2019 ICC Cricket World Cup, setting a new world record.

Test Match Attendance Record: An estimated crowd of 465,000 saw India lose to Pakistan by 46 runs at Eden Gardens, Calcutta (now Kolkata), India, on 16–20 February 1999.

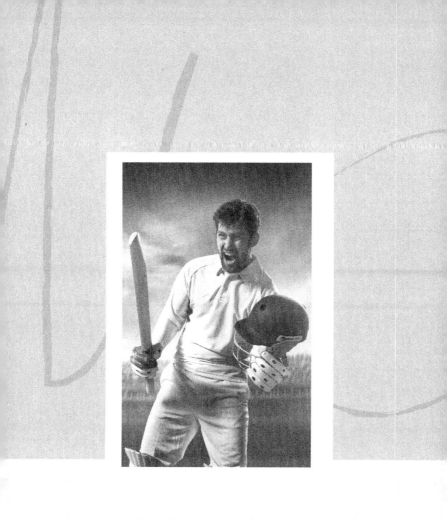

"Cricket is a religion
in India, and the
stadium is our temple."

SOURAV GANGULY

As we reach the end of "The Little Book of Cricket Excuses," we trust that you've enjoyed this collection as a reminder that Cricket is more than just winning matches. It's about the camaraderie on the field, the laughter shared with fellow players, and the enduring memories created long after the bats have been stowed.

While the excuses you've explored within these pages may have brought a smile to your face, let's not overlook that Cricket is a journey of continuous growth and exploration. Every match offers a chance to deepen our grasp of the game and enhance our skills. Sometimes, a missed shot can be a humbling lesson, underscoring that Cricket, like life itself, is filled with mysteries, and true mastery takes time and dedication.

So, the next time you find yourself with a less-than-perfect bowl or an unexpected wide, remember that cricket isn't solely about the score but the entire experience—the thrill of the game, the beauty of the field, and the simple joy of connecting with the sport. And if, in those moments, you discover yourself crafting a witty excuse or sharing a chuckle with fellow players, embrace it as a part of the rich tapestry that makes Cricket such an extraordinary pursuit.

"The Little Book of Cricket Excuses" encourages us to find humor in our Cricket adventures and to cherish the journey as much as the victory. It underscores that even when the win seems elusive, the memories we forge and the bonds we create are what truly matter.

As you close this book, we hope it leaves you with a grin on your face and a renewed enthusiasm for your next match. Remember, Cricket is an expedition full of surprises, and the perfect excuse is just one swing away. Here's to lively shots, memorable bowling, and a treasury of anecdotes to share for years to come.

"Cricket is a battle, and you have to go out there and fight for what you want."

VIRAT KOHLI

Printed in Great Britain
by Amazon